# THROUGH IT ALL

A Survivor's Story of Trusting God
Through Loss, Grief, and Devastation

## Lady Trice

**ILLUMINATION PRESS**

**Atlanta, Georgia**

THROUGH IT ALL

A Survivor's Story of Trusting God Through Loss, Grief, and Devastation

ISBN: 978-1-950681-00-6

Cover and Interior Design by AugustPride, LLC

ILLUMINATION Press
1100Peachtree Street
Suite 250
Atlanta, Georgia 30309
United States

Contact the Publisher:
inspire@illuminationpress.com (678) 744-8128

Contact the Author:
LadyTriceBooks@yahoo.com

# DEDICATION

As I still mourn your death, I know I was blessed to have you for eight months. I'll always remember your first words to me. I owe you so much! When you met me, I was a dying soul. It was you who spoke life back in me and loved me as one of your own daughters. You prayed for me when I refused to pray for myself. Beatrice Smith, forever a mother I will always cherish, I hope I have made you proud.

# ACKNOWLEDGMENTS

I want to thank God for giving me His strength to overcome situations in my life. I thank Him for the peace and healing He gave me during this particular process. I thank Him for just being God and God alone.

I want to thank all of those who pushed and encouraged me not only during my test, but also during the writing process. I thank them for loving me unconditional. I thank them all mostly for believing in my ability to be an "author."

I want to thank my children! Without them I would not have much of a story or a reason to live. Each day we grow together brings joy to my heart. They made me a mother and for that I am a better person.

# TABLE OF CONTENTS

# FOREWORD

*Through It All* is one of those books that you do not want to put down. It keeps you on the edge of your seat, curious as to what is going to happen next—will Faith manifest itself or remain a mere speckle of hope to a soul that is diligently seeking it.

Lady Trice dispels the dark moments of Faith without works is dead and usher's in God's word and manifested Faith by cultivating the soils of her heart, mind and sight. She brings to the forefront that: Mustard seed size faith (Matthew 17:20), Crumb-size faith (Matthew 15:21-28), Unwavering faith (Hebrews 10:23), Active Faith (John 15:7) and Genuine Faith (2 Tim 1:5) manifests itself when you seek the creator through your spiritual eyes and put in the work in the physical realm.

This book is carefully orchestrated by God, through the author to take us on every journey that allows us to experience and feel every hurt, every pain, every tear, every fear, every discouragement, every discomfort, every torment, every heart break and every moment when the manifestation of Faith appeared to let the author down. We also get to experience the rejoicing, the encouragement, the belief, the fasting, the praying, the submission, the renewed relationship with Christ and every moment where Faith manifested itself in the author's life.

This book is a true faith builder that will help you to pick up the pieces of your brokenness and guide you into greater faith and deeper depths in God. *Through It All* provides a true journey of the process on making diamonds and pearls. If the principles and experiences in this book is applied to your life, it will cause an inner faith awakening to be birth within you.

If your life has been in shambles, your faith has been tested and yet to be manifested, then read *Through It All* and allow yourself to embrace every pressurized moment you are faced with to activate and expand your faith until it is manifested. This is a MUST read for every believer who feels like faith has failed them during a time when they needed it to activate most.

Blessings,

*Lady Cheronda S. Walls*

Lady Cheronda S. Walls

Co-Pastor of Levitical International Worship Center, Waldorf, MD

# INTRODUCTION

***Through It All*** is my story.  Real…raw…and 100% authentic.

After hearing about my trials and tribulations over the past few years, so many people told me I should write a book to share my experiences and provide comfort to those who are going through similar circumstances.  At first, I was reluctant, but God showed me that sharing my story was His purpose and His will for what I have been through.

On the pages of this book, I am sharing real life.  It's probably unlike any other book you've ever read.  I don't try to sugar coat anything that happened to me.  From the death of close family members in less than a few weeks apart to losing custody of my children, life threw some nasty curve balls my way, and I share them all in this book. I also share how God brought me through it all.  It wasn't always pretty. My conversations with God were personal and not typically what you would think of when you think of praying to God.  But God and I have developed a very close bond that does not stand on pretense.

As you read, don't look for the standard format of a book.  Don't try to fit this book into the framework of anything you have ever read before.  You are getting a look at my innermost thoughts and feelings, things I have shared with only a few people.  In some places you will read conversations I only had with God.

My prayer is that as you read my story you will come to realize you are not alone. Don't ever let the enemy trick you into believing that your trials and tribulations are bigger than God. No matter what you are going through, know that when you trust God and turn to Him in faith, He will bring you Through It ALL!

# LETTER TO SELF

*Self,*

*How did you allow yourself to get in this place? You allowed yourself to marry a man who did not appreciate your worth, and he took all of the good you did for granted. You felt neglected, and you wanted to escape the physical and mental abuse, so you stepped outside of your marriage in hopes of finding someone to love you. Tired of looking at yourself in the mirror and seeing continued failures and defeat, you decided to get out! After being separated twice you decided to stop trying to make a dying marriage work. No more! It was finally time for you to make a new life for yourself and your three seeds. You definitely thought that if you could not make better choices for yourself than it was best to give your babies the opportunity to grow up in a better atmosphere. A hard decision to make without answers or preparation, you made an unorthodox leap of faith to make yourself homeless while the two oldest children were still in school. You traveled from Maryland to Virginia, slept in your car, peed behind dumpsters, went without food and shelter, all to make a new home in Virginia. Thankful to a few middle and high school friends, you were able to take showers and not have to sleep in your car every night, just most of them. Do you remember the day God said, "Tell her you are homeless and are sleeping in your car"? Thank God, you were obedient and did as you were told, because you know how stubborn and full of pride you can be. That day, that moment, and those words would change your life. God's plan and will for your life was beyond you, but you saw His love unfold for you through the family that adopted you as one of their own. They loved you back to life. No judging, just Jesus! You, baby, finally had a home to come to, food to eat, and a place to bring your kids. Of course, that would not be your resting place though. Oh no, because God had an apartment with your name on it. You had a home for your kids, you were working two jobs, and doing what you love to do best, being a mother. You thought you were about to live your best life, but the sudden storm of reality would soon surface. You never thought or imagined your life would come to this, but here you are.*

*Sincerely,*
*Old Self*

# LETTERS TO GOD

# DEAR GOD

*Did he really just blame me for his failed relationship after telling me that it was his fault because he kept getting caught in lies? Lord, please be a fence all around me. This man is crazy! He jumps into a committed relationship two weeks after our divorce is finalized and then has the audacity to blame me. God, I cannot believe this. He kept the relationship a secret, which is okay with me because it is his life, but I do not appreciate all this hate he is giving to me. It is over the top and a bit overwhelming. Lord, help me to keep my emotions together because I feel my blood pressure rising. I know Your word says to be slow to anger. Yeah, I was too quick to anger on that one. Forgive me Lord, because all my thoughts were unholy. My heart did ache at the thought of him getting a girlfriend so soon. I felt I meant nothing to him. Our marriage lasted almost seven years, and he had a girlfriend two weeks later. What does he say? "I wasn't looking for it." For real? I knew his "ministry" thing was going to be a mess. God, help me to not care because divorcing him was the best thing I could do for my kids and myself. But God, why was he so nice and loving to her in six months and treat me like trash for over six years? You are right God, it does not matter! I need to focus on making sure the kids are okay and are adjusting to the changes they are enduring through the divorce. Keep my heart pure, God. Continue to work on me as a person and a mother.*

*Sincerely,*
*A frustrated woman*

# DEAR GOD

*Gggggoooodddddd!*

*Court…court…mediation…and now, more court!*

*I AM SO OVER IT ALL!!!!*

*Every time I turn around this dude has me back in court. He is mad about everything. Whhhyyyy?*

*I will never understand his reasoning, nor his thought process. It makes absolutely no sense. I am trying to make sense of it all, and every time I try, I come up with a smaller IQ. I know he wants me to fail, but I refuse to do that. You created me to be a mother to these children. You entrusted me with their lives, and I intend to make You proud. Seriously though, Jesus, I am tired of court. Please let this man go get another girlfriend to occupy his time. He has way too much time on his hands. I am over here raising a family while he is busy going to the courthouse.*

*Lord, give me the STRENGTH of Samson.*

*Lord, I pray for a sound mind so I will make sound decisions. My kids are depending on me.*

*Sincerely,*
*Rebuilding my IQ*

# DEAR GOD

*I do not understand what is going on with my life right now. I am tired of this back and forth to court. I just want to raise my children and be the best mother to them. Is all of this unnecessary drama my karma for not being a great wife?*

*This is too much God!*

*This man is too much.*

*I divorced him so that he could have a better life, find his queen, and let me go. I wanted us to both be happy and raise our children in healthier environments. This man that I once shared my life with and gave three beautiful children told me he hates me. He told me I am nothing to him.*

*He is so disrespectful to me even in front of our kids. Please shield their hearts and minds. I know I am paying for my mistakes, but I am still tired. I thought I left all that craziness and foolishness in the divorce—I was wrong! I still feel married to this man, and I definitely should not. I do not know what's worse, the marriage or the current situations.*

*God, I need You. I cannot do this without You. I am trying to keep my sanity and not lose my mind, but it is hard. I need Your strength and guidance. I need Your peace, Your love, and even more of Your strength.*

*I need you Lord!*

*Sincerely,*
*Your disturbed child*

# DEAR GOD

*Really?*

*What is the problem now?*

*I just cannot win. I cannot catch a break. We are still arguing about irrelevant things. I just want to be a mother. I am not a bad mom. He should be happy that he has children by someone who loves and provides for them, but no, he can't see beyond his hatred.*

*Now, he is fussing about not wanting to pay child support. I personally do not see the issue, but he says I want to sit at home and be lazy. God, I am not lazy, nor will I be sitting at home. The amount he will be ordered to give is not enough for me to be home anyway. So, even though I was a little offended, that statement was laughable. I have been working two jobs for a long time even while married to him, and he has the nerve to call me lazy?*

*God, do You remember that I am the same woman who gave birth and went back to work the day after I was released because he could not afford to pay all the bills? God, You made me in that season, though. I should not have been back at work that soon. God, I thank You for Your protection and covering. Regardless if he pays child support or not God, I do not depend on him. You are my provider and way maker. I trust You. I recognize where my help comes from.*

*Sincerely,*
*I am grateful*

# DEAR GOD

*I NEED YOU JESUS!*

*Why does this man think that he can run my household and his? Oh no Lord, he had his moment where he held that title and it was an epic fail. That time has passed. Now he is trying to negotiate claiming my kids for his taxes. That is ridiculous!*

*He only sees our kids as dollar signs. Then he says we should file together, and he will keep $4k and he will give me $3k. Who made him a tax preparer? How does he know how much we will get back? Why is he getting back more than me? Why does he say he will give me $3k like it is his money to give?*

*Whew! There goes my IQ again.*

*I do not understand this logic. God, he does not even want to pay child support, but he wants to benefit from them? Lord, I pray for his mind. I pray for my mind too, because this mind is not like Yours currently.*

*Sincerely,*
*Single mother of 3*

# DEAR GOD

*It is me again!*

*Why is he so evil to me? How is it he can be so happy knowing all the pain he is causing me? He is torturing me, God. He said he would never take my kids away from me. We both cried over the phone that night. I remember it like yesterday but look at where we are now. My kids are gone, and this is one more lie to add to all the other ones he has already spoken. I am not a bad mother. I do not curse. I do not drink wine around my children. I always try to make sure I protect their peace. I do not allow different people to enter their lives, especially guys.*

*I learned from my own misfortunes. Therefore, I am very sensitive to their well-being. How could I have allowed this to happen, God? All for a job? Trying to be there for everyone has failed me. This man is laughing at me. I feel defeated and I am at a loss. I just want to die. Maybe that would be best for my kids because what type of woman, mother am I? I put my job before my kids thinking I needed that money to provide for them. Now, I can't provide for them because they are no longer in my care. God, how could I be so stupid? Why did I let him win? This is my fault, my failure, and I will have to live with this for the rest of my days!*

*Will my kids hate me? What will they think of me? How will I face them? Do they know that I love them? Please let them know that I love them.*

*Sincerely,*
*In my brokenness*

JUNE 28, 2018

On Sunday, June 24, 2018, I reached out to my ex-husband stating that I was starting a new job, and I would not be at court on Thursday, June 28, 2018. Of course, that phone call was a bust and ended not as intended. I was trying to tell him the changes we needed to make to our Parent Agreement documentation.

He started an argument with me, and I hung up. I called back to talk to the kids, and he refused me the opportunity to speak to my children. He told me that I was on his time. At that moment I had not seen or spoken to my kids for ten days, as they were with their dad on summer vacation.

On Thursday, June 28, 2018, I was torn all day. Feeling extremely weird. I did not attend court that day. I was over the whole court "thing." Going to court just to get another date. Too much! Losing money while wasting time. I was not for all of that that day. I needed to provide for my kids and keep a roof over their heads, so I went to work. Every hour counts and every dollar matters; especially since relying on their dad for help was not going to happen.

Later that same day, I drove to Maryland. I paid on the kids' lay-a-way at Kmart, bought clothes from Rainbow, and went to Walmart to buy their shoes. I did all of this because my ex-husband had complained about the condition of our sons' shoes. Even though the kids had been with him for two weeks, he had not taken the opportunity to buy him new shoes. Really my dude? Instead, he waited until I arrived, which was fourteen days later. I didn't complain, though. That's why I was work.

So I can provide everything my children need. I took the shoes to my son, redid my daughters' hair, and went back home.

All the while I am doing all of these things, my ex-husband says nothing about what happened in court. He knew I would not be at court and he also knew that I would be down to visit the kids on that day. It amazes me that he went about business as usual. He allowed the girls to stay overnight with me at my mom's house, but not my son. At the time it didn't make sense to me. Then, the next day, when he came to pick up the girls, he walked away with his head down. Was that guilt or shame? I have no idea. I noticed, but I did not question his strange behavior.

I remember the day as if it were yesterday. I had a few free hours between my two jobs that day, and I decided to visit a friend at work. When I got to her job, I realized she was off that day. Sitting in the parking lot trying to determine what to do next, something in my spirit told me to contact my ex-husband again and ask him about the court appointment I missed. I had been asking him about it for weeks and he never answered me. This time when I emailed him about it, he responded, "It is not my responsibility to tell you, you should have been at court."

Okay buddy! I definitely should have been at court, I agree, but it was partially his responsibility to inform me, especially since I never received anything from the court.

I decided to fight through my anxiety and drove to the courthouse to find out what was going on with my children and why their dad was so secretive and not answering any of my questions or concerns.

I walked into the clerk's office, gave her the information she needed. She printed out the papers and handed them to me. Every word I read pierced me in my heart. It felt as if I was dying. It was like that Lauren Hill lyric, "killing me softly with his words." Only it wasn't "softly" at all.

I burst out into tears. The tears flowed like a river. I paced the floor reading the summary of notes over and over again until the tears burned my eyes. What I was reading was literally suffocating me. The clerk's office seemed as if it were closing in on me. I began to get light headed and panicky. It was as if the walls were enclosing on me. When I missed the court date on June 28, the judge awarded sole custody of my children to their father.

How could this happen? It was one court date. It wasn't right. It made NO SENSE!

How could I have lost custody of my children?

I had to fix this and fast.

I turned to the clerk and asked her what I could do to reverse the decision.

"Unfortunately," the clerk told me, "You may have

missed the deadline to do an appeal." That was another piercing to my heart, but she said, "Do you want to try anyway?"

Of course, I wanted to try. I thought back over the past few weeks. Was this why my ex-husband had refused to answer my questions about the court date over the past two weeks?

I walked out the clerk's office with my appeal documents and information for a legal aid office I could contact. (I was informed that an appeal would not be considered without a lawyer.) I got myself together as much as I could and walked out of that courthouse with a heaviness I cannot adequately explain.

I had so many emotions flowing within me. I was experiencing hurt, anger, confusion, betrayal, shame, disappointment, and frustration, all at the same time. I had never encountered or even heard of a scenario like this before, so I did not know what to do or how to prepare for the things to follow.

The missed court date, the consequence, and the confusion.

When I made it back to my car, I started making calls immediately. I called five of the closest people to me. With each call I became more and more desperate to be comforted. I'm sure I sounded hysterical and didn't make much sense. The emotions that were taking over me had me sobbing beyond my control. I was basically cry screaming.

I called my friend who was in the middle of cutting her grass. I scared the life out of her because I was screaming and crying hysterically. She never heard me like that before. I told her to meet me at my home. She said, "Get yourself together so you can drive home. I will meet you there and we will figure this out."

I called my brother and he cried with me. He helped to endure my pain and the tears I couldn't shed, he did for me. He finally said, "Sis everything is going to be fine. I know you are hurting right now, but you have to be strong for those babies. They need you now more than ever."

A little while later, my friend arrived at my home and she took over. She was the strength I needed, and I am forever grateful for her. She told me to take the day off from my second job because we were going to get a lawyer that day. She drove me to the lawyer's office, I filled out the paperwork, and then it was the waiting game from there. Waiting on the lawyer's return call seemed as if it took forever, and all the while I waited, I was miserable and in constant torment, wondering if everything was really going to work out. It was several agonizing days before I found out the lawyer agreed to represent me.

YOU FORGOT
ABOUT ME!
(I STILL LOVE YOU...)

**God: You forgot about me!**

*Me: So, You are punishing me by taking my kids away from me.*

**God: No, I am not punishing you. I had to get your attention.**

*Me: My kids were the only way to do that, (Tears began to flow) I am so sorry Lord, please forgive me.*

**God: You understand now. Your kids are your life and in the midst of your working and providing for them you forgot about Me. You stopped praising Me and they were who I know I could use to get you to remember Me. I am not punishing you. I just wanted you to know that I still love you.**

*Me: Well God, where do we go from here? What am I to learn from all of this?*

**God: We are going to rebuild your faith and trust in Me. You will learn to lean and depend on Me. You will experience scriptures and live by and through them. You will hear My voice again.**

*Me: I will definitely need You, God, to see me through this.*

**God: I will be with you every step of the way, you just have to trust and believe.**

*Me: Your will be done! Amen*

If only you could understand how bad I felt knowing that I allowed life to let me get so far away from God. I was brought back to my senses when He spoke, "You forgot about me." All I could do was humble myself and cry in shame. I know who God is. I read His word, attended church, experienced His power, and had a relationship with Him. Yet, somehow, I had gotten to the point where I was not even acknowledging Him on a daily basis. The shame I endured when He said, "I had to get your attention." To this day, I still tell the Lord that I am sorry. I also make sure that I take out time each day to be about Him.

God definitely stayed with me every step of the way. I heard His voice so clearly, there was no mistaking it. On the days I felt like I couldn't take any more upset or pain, He encouraged me and strengthened my spirit. There were even times when He sent specific strangers to cross my path and also encourage me. Thank God for those "angel" strangers, for they truly blessed me and loved on me. God divinely designed people just for me during that season of my life. To the world around me it was summer time, but my personal season was winter. (My internal and external seasons will be explained and revealed in God's Purpose.)

# GOD'S PURPOSE!
## (SEPTEMBER 18, 2018)

*"For I know the thoughts that I think toward you, saith the Lord, thoughts of peace, and not of evil, to give you an expected end."*
• •Jeremiah 29:11, KJV • •

**God: There is a purpose for all of this!**

*Me: Yeah? (doubtful)*

**God: Trust that everything is working for your good.**

*Me: I do believe everything happens for a reason.*

**God: Your spirit interceded on your behalf. I heard your heart and felt the pain in your struggle.**

*Me: I just want better for my kids. To be able to do things for and with them.*

**God: Your debt was above your financial ability. You were killing yourself, working two jobs, no days off, and still not getting ahead. I saw your frustration. So, I allowed this to happen for a purpose.**

*Me: What purpose, God? I don't quite see what You see. I need more clarity.*

**God: Faith without works is dead! I am giving you the opportunity to work.**

*Me: ………*

After being unsuccessful at getting an earlier court date to resolve this custody battle before the kids had to start school, I had to wait until September 18, 2018. I was so upset because I wanted my kids back so badly, but God had a different plan that I had no choice but to surrender to. His will, not mine, right? Of course!

I missed the first day of school, the opportunity to pick out school outfits, and back to school hair do's. My then three-year-old missed her opportunity to go to school full time because her dad decided his mom and daycare were better. I tried to explain to him how a Monday through Friday school experience would benefit her better and she would be learning all day. He denied that request, so she lost her spot. Immediately, hurt rushed through me, and there was nothing I could do about it.

On top of her not being able to go to school, I was not allowed to visit my two oldest kids at school either. I emailed their dad asking about school, and I asked him if I could take the kids to school on their first day, anything to cope with this internal pain I was trying to endure. His response was, "They have to ride the bus!"

I thought that response was ridiculous. I would have respected any other comment but that one.

On September 3, 2018 I stayed with a friend so I could be closer to the kids my children's school the next morning.

I went to the local Food Lion and bought Lunchables and candy for the kids because I had promised them that I would. I told their dad that I had them and that I would drop them off to him. Again, his response was ridiculous.

He said, "I don't need you to do that I already took care of that for them. They are good."

Instantly my anxiety went up, and I ended up leaving the bag of food on his door.

September 4, 2018, the first day of school! I wasn't happy, but I wanted to see my kids and let them know that I was there to support them. I was late to work because I didn't want to miss their first day. When I arrived at the school, I had to wait in the office. I asked to speak with the principal who informed me that I was prohibited from seeing my kids without written permission from their dad. Permission to see the kids I carried and gave life to? Are you serious right now? I couldn't believe it, didn't want to believe that. I cried so much in her office that morning. So not only did I miss the first day of school, but I was late to work also, and needed permission to see my own kids. Wait… what??? That was the longest two-and-a-half-hour drive of my life. I had to tell myself to stop crying because I needed to focus on driving. The feeling I felt that day remains unexplainable.

Finally, September 18, 2018 had arrived. I was so nervous and still so ready for my babies to come home. I was thinking it was still early enough in the year that they wouldn't fall behind. I walked in that courtroom just to find that November 30, 2018 would be the actual hearing. Inner thought, "Are you serious right now?" That felt like an eternity away. I had to have a conversation with God.

*Me: Okay God, the date got pushed back by two weeks. There must be a reason. Is there more for me to do that I would need more time?*

**God: You will see why.**

*Me: I am trusting in You!*

**God: ............**

After getting my feelings all the way hurt, and not getting my kids back, I knew that I needed to get my house in order. Several changes were necessary to make. September !8, 2018 was a changing point in my life I will forever remember and be thankful for.

**God: You are tired of being in debt this I know.**

*Me: Yes God!*

**God: For this reason, this is the purpose for losing custody of your kids.**

*Me: To get out of debt?*

**God: Amongst other things, but yes. This is your season to become debt free. Financially stable, a**

**good steward over your money, and new beginnings.**

*Me: You really have heard my heart. Just wish my kids weren't the sacrifice.*

**God: Without your kids present you will be able to work whenever and however long you need to accomplish specific goals.**

*Me: God be with me! You have given me a short window to achieve all of this.*

To achieve this goal, I went from working two jobs to now working three jobs. God didn't lie when He said that I would have to work. I knew it was God's will for this third job when I received the text stating, "Do you still want to work here because four people just quit." I had never been a waitress before, but I am a fast learner. Plus, I would do anything to get my kids back and fulfill God's purpose, so I started the job with no worries. This job came right on time as I was already short on money for rent for that month. I was so thankful to God. He came through right on time.

From September's court hearing to November's court hearing I was given seventy-three days to get out of debt. Two months and two weeks to get my whole life together, to get out of debt and increase my credit score.

No pressure, right?

Wrong!

The good part is—I worked so much the time went by faster than I anticipated. I had a total of five debts to focus on. Four out of five of the debts were paid off completely in October and the last bill was paid off November 30, 2018, the day I was scheduled to go back to court.

I am a person who believes in numbers and colors. It took me forty-three days to erase four debts. Forty-three represents hard working, and diligent. It is a sign that an angel is providing guidance, inspiration, and the clarity needed to achieve any creative goals. It is a message of encouragement.

In total, it took me seventy-three days to delete or cancel all my debt. Seventy-three refers to the manifestation of desires and being on the right path. As I was able to sit back and reflect on how long it took me to get everything done, I was truly amazed. The meanings of the numbers were so spot on. How could I not rejoice knowing that God's word did not return void. The conversations we had, the words He spoke to me, how I was able to see that this was all a part of His plan, and how I was in the divine will of God. It was all starting to make more sense.

# OCTOBER
## (DEATH-TOBER)

I guess life didn't have me crazy and emotional enough already.

I was still trying to put the pieces of my life back in order and figure out what God's plan was, then BOOM

*"Your uncle died, I just thought you should know."*

I was so disturbed by how that information was given to me that it took me la while to process the message. I remember calling my brother and telling him to never let that person call me and relay messages to me ever again. I was so mad at that person for approaching a delicate subject so coldly. After I stopped replaying those words in my mind, I broke down and cried. I was truly disturbed at the news. I was not expecting my uncle's death. The last time I saw him was in May, at the funeral of my cousin, who had died in a tragic motorcycle accident. It was an extreme amount of pain to bear considering all the factors. I had suffered enough heartache over the last several months, so I thought.

My uncle's funeral was on Friday, October 12, 2018. The funeral services were held in Danville, Virginia. The service was nice, my brother did the eulogy. The soloist was unable to make it, so Pop Pop, my grandfather, appointed me to sing in her place. I was a nervous wreck, but I never tell Pop Pop no. At the end of my uncle's service Pop Pop told us, my brother, his first-born grandson, and me, his second born grandchild and first granddaughter, that he was proud of us.

After the funeral, life went back to normal. Well, as "normal" as possible with all the challenges happening in my life at the time.

I went back to working crazy hours trying to stay on target with my own personal goals. I had just arrived to work and was at my cubicle in the work room getting ready to meet my student in class. I received a text from my brother at 8:30 am, "Trice, are you at home or work?"

I knew that it couldn't be good news. My brother and I don't normally talk at that hour. That text sent off a negative alert, so I called him. I said, "What's wrong?" He said," Dad called me this morning and said Pop Pop died."

I remember standing in the middle of the floor stuck. I kept repeating, "My Pop Pop died?" Every time I repeated those words the tears began to build up until I could no longer hold them. I hung up the phone and began to go into a panic attack. I had to breathe and get myself together if I wanted to make it through that day at work. I did make it through my whole work day, barely. I cannot recall how many mini breakdowns I had. Thankful to co-workers who loved on me and let me cry.

I took the life of my Pop Pop for granted. He was eighty-two when he died, but I was expecting him to live to be at least one hundred. I thought I had a lot more time with him. I seriously joked with him how he would walk me down the aisle once I found the man created for me. I told him I didn't care how long it took us to get to the alter as long as he was there with me.

"Bring the cane and/or walker Pop Pop. We will slow stride our way up there."

I loved that man so much! Out of all his grandchildren, I was the only one who shared his birth month.

The last time I saw my Pop Pop was on October 12, 2018 at my uncle's, his baby boy's, funeral. Three days later on October 15, 2018 my Pop Pop was found dead. Had I known that would have been my last encounter with him, I would have held him longer. I would have kept telling him how much I loved and appreciated him, anything, or something, I am not sure. I just was not ready for him to leave me. I know that is selfish, but oh well. That was my Pop Pop, my dude, my heart, my love, and he is irreplaceable, one of a kind. The reason I am here, the patriarch of the Sherman family. I was and will always be proud to be his granddaughter.

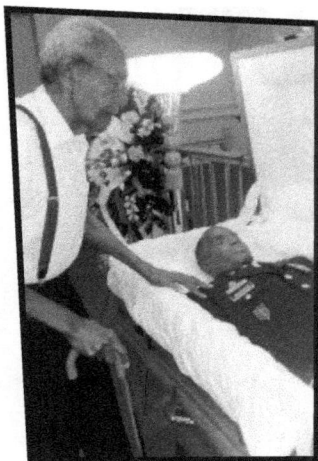

# DEAR GOD

## (THE PRAYER!)

*I really am at a total loss as of right now. I am not sure what is to be taught or learned through this. I am reflecting back on the events that started in April. April, I no longer enrolled in my college courses due to financial aid, that was upsetting to me, and I was doing so well. May, Amire celebrated his thirtieth birthday and died three days later. I was so heart broken when his sister sent me an inbox message on May 21, 2018 at 9:25 am saying, "Amire passed away last night." I thought she was joking. I responded, "You playing?" When she said, "No I'm so serious," I couldn't stop crying. I was like not my baby. I was at work and had to walk the track to get myself together. June, I missed the court date. July, I found out that I lost custody of my children and basically had no rights to them. August, it had been over a month since the last time I was able to spend time with my kids. September, I went to court in hopes to have my babies come home. That court date was just to get another court date two months away.*

*Now, we're in October and my only uncle on my dad's side has died and a week later my Pop Pop dies. How is one to bear all of this? This is over the top. I can't take too much more pain. It has been so much for me to carry, to endure, to deal with.*

*When will I catch a break?*

**God: I am giving you what you can carry.**

*Me: What, God?*

**God: I will not put on you more than you can bear.**

*Me: Really? 'Cause I feel weighed down, defeated, and hopeless.*

**God: Remember, I am trusting you to overcome.**

*Me: I don't see what You see God. I do not understand your reason.*

**God: All you need to understand is that all things are working for your good. Praise Me through your pain.**

God, I thank You and I give You all the praise. Not only do You know my heart, You see it. Every tear I have cried has felt like blood was pouring out of my heart. You have caught, bandaged, and covered my tears with Your own blood. For You died that I may have life and have it more abundantly. I trust Your will for my life. Although I do not understand everything I experience and go through, I understand that you are with me every step pf the way. You will never leave me nor forsake me. You are my strong tower, my strength, my way maker. You are the God of gods, the King of kings, you are my God, the "I am that I am."

It is written that many are called, but few are chosen.

God, I thank You for being among the chosen. You have chosen me, and you have called me daughter. I stand taller knowing that I can be bold in You. I give You honor and glory. I may feel defeated right now, but faith says, "I will win." I just need to seek Your face. Purify my heart, renew my mind, create in me a clean heart, Oh God. Let me hear Your voice. Speak to my heart and encourage me through Your word. Let me see what You see. Let me surrender to Your will. Make me a better me because of all that I have been through. Don't allow bitterness to enter in my heart, but in brokenness bless me. Heal me from past and present pains. Protect my heart, show me who is for me or against me. Teach me how to deal with people. Allow me to be slow to anger. Rebuild my spirit that I may grow my wings like a butterfly. That I can soar like an eagle. So I can be as loving as a dove. I am a work in progress. I fail at times, but there is no failure in You.

Give me clarity. Reveal my purpose, let me walk into my destiny. All things are working for my good. I am more than a conqueror and I am made a victor because you have already fought my battles. All I have to do is walk victoriously. God, I thank You for Your love. I thank You for Your grace, guidance, direction, and protection. I owe you my life!

Where would I be without Your faithfulness and patience?

I know I make You mad and get on Your nerves, but You are always near, waiting for me to get my act right. I can never repay You for all that You have done and continue to do. I am grateful. Protect my babies' hearts and minds. Continue to anoint them with Your oil. Be with them and disperse their angels. Protect them while they are at school and open up their understanding. I pray for my kids' dad. Send him love. Heal his hurting heart. In Jesus' name it shall be done.

Sincerely,

Burdens are broken

I love how God interrupted my sad prayer and spoke to me. In the midst of my prayer, He showed up and encouraged me. After our conversation, my prayer changed. It was bolder and proves that when God shows up things have to be different. I thank God for the confidence and boldness He restored back into me. God said, "No pity parties when work is to be done." Pray with faith not by the factors that are weighing you down.

# NOVEMBER 30, 2018

## (IT HAS BEEN ESTABLISHED!)

The new court date had seemed to be so far away, but it came so quickly. I fasted twelve hours a day for three days before the court date. I had not done that in years. Yes, it was a struggle, but I had no other choice but to press. I had a mission to accomplish that involved regaining physical custody of my children. Therefore, my attitude was, "God, I won't leave until You bless me," or the cliché "by all means necessary."

If I said that I was fine and unbothered that would be a straight up lie. I was tormented in fear. I was asked, "What if you don't get the kids back? What will you do with the clothes you bought?" Those words came from someone I trusted with my life, I loved that person dearly. I would have never expected that particular person to say such hurtful words to me, especially when I needed encouragement and love during that time. I will admit that those words broke me.

On Thursday, November 29, 2018, I went on my Facebook page and added this prayer to my stories:

*"November 29, 2018*

*I want to thank You for all You have done for me. As I pray in faith and not in doubt, I know that You will fight my battle for me. Align my thoughts and ways with Yours. Order my steps, lead as I follow. Guide my path while guarding my heart. Remove any and all anger, replace with a renewed spirit, mind, and Your perfect peace. Thank You for Your undeniable power. I rebuke anxiety, shortness of breath, fear, distractions, negativity, and doubt. For I understand a table was prepared for me in the presence of my enemies, but You assure me that You are with me every step of the way. You are my strength, my strong tower, my courage, and my victor. Bridle my tongue so that You can speak for and through me. Restore into what was lost. For I am trusting that mountains in my life are about to be removed. I praise You for all things. Thank You for my trails, tests, testaments, disappointments, sacrifices, dreams, and visions. Thank You for speaking to me. I am so grateful that all things are working together for my good in spite of what it looks like. You told me that I could bear it all. Yes, weeping and many tears have been shed, but my morning, my awakening is soon to come forth. I am walking in your joy and peace. You are shaking and disturbing my atmosphere to make room for my overflow of favor and blessings. Thank You for favor. Let Your will be done. Let me fully accept Your will for my life. Open up the doors You see fit for me. Let the words of my mouth be acceptable in Thy sight, oh Lord, my Lord, in Jesus' name. It is so. Amen!*

*Your Daughter"*

It was a pretty lengthy prayer, but you can still grasp the point and purpose of the prayer. I was unable to say these words aloud, so writing my prayer was therapeutic. Once I got past the first few sentences, the rest of the words just flowed as if my spirit was interceding for me. After writing that prayer God said, "Now watch my power tomorrow in the court room."

The day had finally arrived!

A nervous wreck I was.

November 30, 2018 was the determination of my fate. Would I get my children back or not? I was scared to death and feared what the judge may say. God had to remind me that is was not up to the judge, that He had the final say.

I drove to the courthouse for an early meeting with my lawyer. As I was walking to the building, I hung my head down in shame. God immediately spoke to me saying, "Walk with your head held high, you have no reason to be ashamed." It was as if a hand came from out of nowhere and lifted my chin. That was the confirmation I needed to reassure me that God was with me.

My courtroom experience is one I hope to never experience again. Too many mixed emotions. The kids' dad who is always on time was nowhere in sight. No one had heard from him. The judge recessed for ten minutes to give him a chance to get there. Even after that delay he never showed. That didn't keep me from being on trial though. It was my case and I had to present reasons why I left my kids' dad, why did I move to Virginia, how did they adapt to the change, why didn't I show up to court on June 28, 2018? I was tortured with question after question for the longest thirty-five to forty minutes of my life and it was mostly my lawyer questioning me. When the judge did question me, I was thinking he is not going to let my kids come home. He even questioned the GAL (guardian ad litem) as to why she let this situation happen without a continuance.

The people that I was in contact with during this unfortunate situation kept asking me what happened. Why did dad get custody so quickly? It just did not make sense. We live in two different states, I wasn't aware dad was filing for custody, there were no known and/or stated reasons as to why they should leave me. Just the whole situation of how everything happened and the way that it did was absolutely crazy. I was happy to hear the judge felt the same way.

This is what was written on June 28, 2018 for the new order I appealed.

## 2. CUSTODY/PARENTING TIME/VISITATION

MOTHER FAILED TO APPEAR AFTER ACTUAL NOTICE. MOTHER'S MOTIONS TO AMEND VISITATION IS DISMISSED.

THE GAL REPORTS THAT THE MOTHER KNEW OF THE FATHER'S MOTION FOR CUSTODY AND ALSO WAS ADVISED BY THE GAL THAT SHE NEEDED TO APPEAR AT COURT. THE FATHER PROVIDED TESTIMONY ABOUT HIS CONCERNS. THE COURT TOOK JUDICIAL NOTICE OF THE MARYLAND CIRCUIT COURT OF CHARLES COUNTY, MARYLAND CONTEMPT CHARGE ENTERED ON 02/28/2018. THE FATHER TESTIFIED UNDER OATH THAT THE MOTHER HAS FAILED TO COMPLY WITH THAT ORDER. THEREFORE, BASED UPON THE EVIDENCE AND TESTIMONY, THE FATHER IS GRANTED SOLE LEGAL AND PHYSICAL CUSTODY OF THE CHILD. MOTHER MAY HAVE SUPERVISED VISITATION OF THE CHILD IN MARYLAND AT THE FATHER'S DISCRETION UNTIL FURTHER ORDER OF THE COURT.

When the judge was ready to decide my new fate, I saw God's shekinah glory enter into that court room. My eyes were so foggy it was hard to concentrate on the words he was speaking. I heard God say, "This is the moment where you see Me work."

The judge's final words were, "Ma'am go get your kids and good luck."

My lawyer's final words after we walked out of that courtroom were, "As soon as you get this new order, you go and get your kids. I don't care if you have to pick them up from school, his house or whatever. You get law enforcement involved if necessary, but you get your kids and bring them back home."

I cried so much that day, so happy that God's will found favor in me. I could not praise Him enough. Knowing that I was not found nor faulted as being an insufficient mother, that the legal system had failed me. That meant a lot to me. I had truly doubted my ability and was so angry with myself and those words were what I needed to hear to regain my peace. Thankful to my best friend who was at court with me and was there to not only share in my great news but allowed me to cry. She said, "I knew you would get them back, you are a great mother and they need to be with you. This news is the best birthday gift. Now go home and get some rest."

Life was finally about to get back to what I found normal.

Again, I spoke too soon! Optimism can be worse than karma sometimes.

# THE GOOD,
# THE BAD,
# THE SCARY
# OF
# DECEMBER 2018

I hadn't received or heard anything further from the courts. My lawyer advised that I physically go to the court house and see if they have anything. I did that and to my liking, my new documentation was ready, and I could receive a copy. I went on Friday, December 7, 2018 and the judge signed off on the new order on Tuesday, December 4, 2018. I finally had the papers that validated the final judgment on November 30, 2018.

Saturday, December 8, 2018 was a special day. My youngest daughter turned four. Now mind you I could have been mean and got my kids and she would have spent her birthday with me as she always has, but I did not. Dad had sent me an email stating that he already planned a party for her, so I didn't want her to be sad about missing her party. I didn't want her to be mad at me. I took her feelings into consideration over my own. That was the first birthday I ever missed for any of my children. Never again!

This is the email sent to dad on Sunday, December 9, 2018.

"I think the best transition for the kids is to wait until Winter Break. That will allow them time to say goodbye to teachers and friends. Also, that should allow the teachers to make any necessary reports about their academic progress/struggles, such as extra help needed and/or growth. This will give more than enough time for Mrs. DG to do their school withdrawals. I will be at BaE on Wednesday,

December 19, 2018. I do not know where Azariah will be, so I will need that information unless you are going to meet me at the school. I will let you know a specific time closer to date.

. . . . . . . . . . . .

If you have not received the new order by now, let me know and I will make sure you get a copy."

No response to this email until five days later.

"Good morning

I tried calling several times to reach out to you about this transition, I received your email after reviewing it, not sure if you are saying you want them on 19th, that will be taking them out of school early, the winter break doesn't start until 21st of December, their education is very important to me and they still have programs going on that week that they really want to be a part of, Friday December 21 is 2hr dismissal at school we can set up time after school to meet. This also gives Azariah time with her holiday activities in daycare and with her head start teacher.

This email is only addressing when you are picking them up on Friday December 21, 2018 after school.

Thank you."

As an educator you could imagine that run on sentence really bothered me. All those commas, and no punctuation.

It took me a few moments to focus on what the content of what was being said. I was reading his late response with the mind that this guy is still trying to dictate to me when I can get my kids. As far I was concerned those days ended on November 30. He still had to be in control. I was certainly not worried about parties and activities. Education wasn't that deep or serious so close to Winter Break, I should know. I have worked for the school system for five years by this time. He was going to have to come better than that to convince me to wait two more days because that was not happening.

My response to his email.

"I was told I could get them at any time. I could have come and got them Friday, December 7, 2018, but decided not to mess up your birthday party plans for Azariah. I am also told that if you are not willing to comply to call law enforcement. I am getting them on December 19, 2018. They will just have to miss some things. Also, the kids have dental appointments on December 21, 2018 at 9:30 am. Please don't make this bigger than it has to be. Let Mrs. DG know that I will be at Ba to get my kids on Wednesday, December 19, 2018. I just need to know who and where to get Azariah from. I am going by the Hanover County school winter break and December 19, 2018 is the last day of school."

Straight to the point. I had already had to reschedule

that dental appointment once before. I refused to do it a second time. No better time to go while I didn't have to take more time off from work.

On December 19, I arrived at the school early, got the papers I needed, drove two hours back to Virginia, and enrolled my babies in school. Best feeling ever! I wanted to make sure that on January 3, 2019 they would be at school. You better know that they were. New clothes, new shoes, and hair styled, baby. I know it wasn't the actual first day of school, but I made sure to take pictures as though it was. (I refused to miss anymore memorial moments.)

God, what is going on? This cannot be true! I couldn't believe I woke up to read an email that stopped my heart.

"Friday, December 28, 2018 at 9:28 AM

On Friday December 21, the courts issued a new order, which has suspended the current order that you have now, I still have custody of the children they are still staying in Maryland and are still enrolled at bae, which they will be back in school on January 2nd which they are excited about, if you can possible I really would like for you to call them more frequently during the week so you can hear about there day at school and there progress in class, and also I am willing to download a video app so you can see them so you can see them during the week and also to see there progress on homework and etc. I already have video on WhatsApp for facetime on my cell phone if you have it as well that would be wonderful. Even on your days off if you wanted to go to the school and eat lunch with them the school secretary is already notified and will definitely make sure you can do so. Also if you are available to go with them on there upcoming field trips that would be amazing, I know they would definitely enjoy that.

If you want to them every weekend or the weekends that you are off work please let me know what your schedule is I will definitely make sure that will be ready to spend time with time with you for the weekends. I want you to spend as much time with them as you can so don't worry about on Sundays at 2:30pm to meet at Walmart that is too short of a time we can me by 5pm I like to have to have the kids settled on Sunday nights by 7pm for school the next day.

If you need any further documentation or if you haven't received anything in the mail yet please contact your attorney, I'm quite sure that she will have all information and new order in there office by now.

Have a safe and wonderful new year"

I felt like I did that day I was at the court house reading that a judge gave my kids to their dad. I kept saying, "I can't go through that again, I barely made it through the first time. Oh God, I need You. This makes no sense." I let a lot of time go by. I was contemplating whether or not to respond and if I did, how would I respond? I called my brother, my best friend, and my lawyer in that order. I called my brother so he could pray for my mind. I called my best friend so she could cuss him for me and help me sort out my thoughts and the missing pieces. I called my lawyer to see if this email was legit and have her advise me what the next step would be.

You are probably like wait…what? I had my kids for a week before the court ordered Christmas visitation with dad took place. So, when he emailed me the kids were just supposed to be visiting and spending time with him. That is all. So, imagine my fears, worries, and concerns. Terrified and tormented by my own thoughts. I was definitely in my own head from his words and my own worst enemy.

My lawyer was on vacation, but she did respond, thank God. She said, "Catrice, I brought your case file with me. Are the kids with him visiting? Catrice, he is just trying to get in your head. He has been controlling you for so long he still wants to control you. He is trying to manipulate you. You have to stand up for yourself. He is mad that you got your kids back. He is just going to have to put his big boy pants on. You need to respond to that email."

"Friday, December 28, 2018 at 2:58 PM

There is no new order in place. I find your last email to not only be a threat to keep my children from me, but also an attempt to try and manipulate me to believing false information. Your action will be considered harassment. If need to be I will follow through with a protective order.

Law enforcement will be notified if you violate the court order that has been placed on December 4, 2018. Also, if you keep my kids from me, I will file a Motion for Contempt as well. Which could lead to you being locked up.

I expect to pick up my kids January 1, 2019 at 2:20 pm at Walmart.

Anything referring to legal matters need to be addressed to my lawyer to lawyer. Do not contact me unless it is pertaining to Noadiah, Elijah, an/or Azariah personally."

Four days later, January 1, 2019, I picked up my kids and we went home.

# JANUARY 2019

## (BACK TO REALITY!!!)

On January 2, 2019, we picked out outfits for school, and I did the girls hair. Best moment and feeling of my life. Back to doing what I love most, being a full-time mother. This day is a day I embedded into my memory and heart for the rest of my days. I remember Azariah said, "Mom, dad is mad at you. You want us and he wants us. You fought for us!" I was stunned to hear these words from my four-year-old. I do not have these types of conversations with her. I was disturbed some.

"You fought for us," touched me to my soul.

I had asked God and wondered what my kids would think. I know God spoke through my baby to let me know that my kids knew that I truly loved them. In my head I said, "Mommy will always fight for her babies. Trust and believe that. With every fiber of my being." Instead, I just listened to her heart enjoying listening to her voice.

On January 3, 2019, back to reality.

I had to adjust my sleep pattern and wake up schedule, but I was more than happy to do that. We woke up and started our day. I didn't let the kids ride the bus that morning because I wanted to meet the teachers. When school was over, I met the kids at the bus stop. I was overwhelmed with joy that my babies were officially back with me. Yes, I did take bus pictures, enjoying the fullness of God's love for me. God turned my situation around. He made my mistake a miracle.

I was a mother on a mission. The month of January was very busy not only for the kids, but me as well. I emailed their teachers to make sure that they would have enough grades for their report cards. I informed them that if necessary, they could send extra work home and I would work with them on the assignments. Their teachers both assured me that they would have enough grades and extra assignments would be unnecessary.

On January 29, 2019, I went to work late. I went to Noadiah's IEP meeting at 8 am and was there for an hour. I then went to work, left work, and got the kids off the bus. After that we went back to Elijah's school to have a parent teacher conference at 3 pm. I was glad to hear their strengths as well as their challenges, so I had a better idea of how to further help them at home.

The first report cards home!

I was a little nervous considering the pressure that was on Noadiah and Elijah. They had maybe a little over three weeks (15 school days) to get grades, but also maintain good scores. Long story short, Noadiah and Elijah both made the AB Honor Roll. Dad had them for about 53 school days and Noadiah had more C's than she had ever had since she started school in September 2014. She had been a B student overall. Imagine my frustrations when I saw those C's when I was told that she was being helped with her homework daily.

The month of January was indeed a blessed month. My new year could not have been better than this. I had custody of my kids again, they were doing well in school, and they adapted very well to all the changes they had experienced over the previous months. The reality shown to me was that I was created to be a mother. God designed me for motherhood, and he trusted me with Noadiah, Elijah, and Azariah's life.

Everything that I do, every decision made is based around and for them, for they are my life. I am responsible for creating an environment that allows them peace and a place they can feel safe. I take motherhood seriously. No longer do I just live for me, I live for them.

"2020 I WILL
PERFECT
YOUR VISION!"

On December 25, 2018, when I got back home from dropping the kids off to spend time with their dad for Christmas, God said, "You need to do a vision board." I was so sad that my kids were back with their dad so soon, but I was court ordered, so I had no choice. That week with them went by so fast. Basically, I had missed them already.

In obedience I started brainstorming specific scriptures and thinking of what pictures I would need to accomplish this goal. That is all I did that day though. It wasn't until February 2, 2019 that I actually started my vision board. February 3, 2019, God said, "Complete the vision today." I completed my vision board and am pretty proud of my work. That was my ordained day to focus on positive affirmations. My vision board would be established in the earth.

*"And the Lord answered me, and said, Write the vision, and make it plain upon tables, that he may run that readeth it."*
• • **Habakkuk 2:2, KJV** • •

From December 25th to January 3rd was nine days. Since I fully believe in the power of numbers, I also counted how many days from when God first mentioned the vision board to me until the day, I completed it in totality. In church I was taught that the number nine meant "completeness." That of course is in short. The number nine has many other significant meanings, but for my particular situation "completeness" is the best answer. God was just speaking to me so much and I enjoyed listening to Him. He was revealing to me my own personally revelations. Amazing!

On February 10, 2019 there was a short clip of my brother's sermon posted on Facebook. I was blessed to be able to hear it. He was speaking of the woman with the issue of blood. Even though our all-knowing, omniscient God understood the woman's troubles, He still had the woman explain her issues. My brother proceeded to mention how her transparency about her issues were not necessarily for God's ears, but the crowd that was present. We understand that hearing increases our faith. When God would therefore heal this lady, the crowd would fully understand the power of God. (This is my personal interpretation and what I received from his sermon.)

It was at that moment my God spoke to my spirit which penetrated my soul. He said, "2020 I will perfect your vision!"

Those words were life changing. Only two months into the new year and God has already promised me that great things would happen for me. Something to look forward to. I adopted His words as my motto for the rest of 2019.

Naturally people have 20/20 vision. It means they can see without the need of glasses or contact lenses. Their vision is not blurred, but clear. I began to praise God off that revelation.

Then I thought about the number twenty and its meaning. Twenty means complete or perfect waiting period. The numbers separated two and zero means balance in spirituality. I said to myself, "God, I have been waiting for some doors to open and some changes to occur in my life. You are encouraging me and reassuring me that in 2020 that those desires will be established as the waiting period would have matured."

Look at God opening up my understanding.

Not only will He give me the desires of my heart, but He is about to increase my spiritual balance. Wow, God really hears my heart. I said, "God. I need a covering. I need to be in church again." He basically told me He was about to give me all that I was asking for. I was in His divine will.

You will have to wait and see what God does for me in 2020. The title of that book will be the same as the title of this chapter. ("2020 I will Perfect your Vision!")

THROUGH IT ALL...

*Dear Old Self,*

*You have surprised yourself and your ability to endure tough situations. You should be proud of yourself. You survived what you thought for sure would kill you. Death hoovered over you, but life was victorious. Remember when you wrote that poem almost eighteen years ago?*

*You didn't understand the reasoning for God putting those words in your spirit, but you remember the urgency to write these words on paper. Now, you have a better understanding of the why. God was telling you that you are one of His chosen children and that you would live through it all. Every test, trial, tribulation, and threat. Every heartbreak, disappointment, argument, and abuse. Through the loss of loved ones, losing custody of your children, being withdrawn from college, and working three jobs to provide for your family. The pain endured, the tears shed, the panic attacks, and anxiety attacks. All the negative things in your life were unto death, but your praise allowed life to win. God was preparing you then with that poem. Those words were written for this moment. You walk with a sense that God is always near. With a confidence in your faith you hold your head up high. Greater appreciation of why God chose you to bear all that He allowed you to. You are an overcomer who overcame the depressions of life. God knew that He could trust you to come out as a conqueror and be a testament of His power and glory. You are a survivor through it all!*

*Sincerely,*

*New improved you*

# I SHALL LIVE AND NOT DIE!

I shall not die
But live
For my flesh will
Die naturally
But my soul
Will live spiritually

I shall not die
But live
For I will serve
The God of Life
And resist the Devil
Of death

I shall not die
But live
For my destiny is far
Above this world
And higher
Than any mountain
I shall not die in Hell
But live in Heaven
There I will praise
God
For death has not won me
But life

# ABOUT THE AUTHOR

Catrice "Lady Trice" Sherman loves being a testament of God's glory. Always ready to encourage those she encounters; Lady Trice doesn't mind being transparent when helping others—her life is as an open book.

Lady Trice is currently a Special Education Instructional Assistant in the Virginia school system. With a dedication to serve and equip the next generation, Lady Trice continues to pursue higher education and will soon earn a dual Bachelor's degree in Early Childhood Education and Special Education from Grand Canyon University.

Lady Trice takes great pride in being the mother of three brilliant children. Noadiah, 8, Elijah, 7, and Azariah, 4, are the reasons she strives for greatness. She is building her life that she may be a positive role model, a great example, and the best mother they could ever hope for.

Lady Trice is an ordinary person who just so happened to listen to the voice of God one day and began to write. Now this ordinary woman is now considered an author. Writing was never in her plan, but God's plan.

**Contact Lady Trice for interviews, book signings, and speaking engagements.**

**LadyTriceBooks@yahoo.com**